Chief of Staff

LEADERS CIRCLE

Presents

Unlocking Your Inner Chief of Staff

Guide to Maximizing Organizational Impact

An illustrated handbook for individuals in Chief of Staff or executive operations roles...

LEIGH FELTON

ISBN: Softcover 9798387311673

Library of Congress Control Number: 1-12397643451

Published through Kindle Direct Publishing, March 2023

www.amazon.com
www.cosleaderscircle.com

Unlocking Your Inner Chief of Staff

Guide to Maximizing Organizational Impact

By LEIGH FELTON

The Ultimate Guide to mastering the Chief of Staff role and taking over the world!

(or at least the chaos in the office) LOL

Leigh Felton

Leigh is a seasoned Chief of Staff, author, public speaker, coach, and responsible innovation & technology equity activist. With over 25 years in the technology industry, and 15 of those as operations executive and Chief of Staff to top CEOs, she has assembled a wealth of knowledge in setting up organizations for success.

In addition to her work in operations and communications, Leigh has led responsible and ethical AI programs, and has passion for ensuring technology benefits all. She also worked in Public Sector as Director of the Business Services Division in the Department of Commerce for Washington State.

Leigh has experience working with and leading executive teams, to create structure, and drive transformational change. Her ultimate goal is to help educate individuals on the importance of integrity, structure, and bringing every employee along to enjoy the ride!

Follow me on LinkedIn
https://www.linkedin.com/in/lefel/

DEDICATION

This book is dedicated to the one person who believed in me more than I even believed in myself. The person who kept pushing me to do more and take my talents to the next level. With lots of love and positive energy your way...

additionally...

This book is also dedicated to all the CEOs I have worked with and for.

Your role is a lonely one. Nothing can intimidate one so powerful, than guessing who is your true ally, or wondering if anyone will instinctively have your back through thick and thin. You want to be seen as a person and respected as a leader.
A deserving COS will do just that, and be a collaborative leader alongside you, amplifying and nurturing the organization as an implementer and strategist.

Please remember, a true partner is one who will be there when you are up, and race to catch you when you're falling. Believing in someone who is authentic, who will look out for you, and who is your eyes and ears to the ground, comes at a cost.
That cost is trust. Have their back as they have yours.

TABLE OF CONTENTS

MEET COSLY!

Written

by Leigh Felton

Edited

by Leigh Felton

Designed

by Leigh Felton

Graphic Compilations

by Leigh Felton

because a COS really does try to do it all!

And Starring
COSLY

as
Leigh Felton

Meet Cosly!

I am a seasoned Business Strategist and Operations Executive, who has spent more than 15 years in the Chief of Staff role supporting CEOs and equivalent.

I have learned a few tricks of the trade and bad habits to break along the way.

COSLY (They/Them)
Operations Extraordinaire and Guide

My Philosophy:

Intersectionality plays a significant role in my life. Recognizing the beauty in all things that shape me, contributes to my career success and life satisfaction.

WELCOME TO THE
CHIEF OF STAFF LEADERS CIRCLE

Unlocking Your Inner Chief of Staff:
Guide to Maximizing Organizational Impact

Why would a brilliant, leader, strategist, and go-to person for the most powerful person in the organization need a handbook?

Come along for the ride and find out!

BUT FIRST...
Please do not continue reading if you do not...
Have a Sense of Humor!
If you haven't developed one, you either have not been a COS for long enough, or have been one for far too long!

WHO IS THIS BOOK FOR?

Well, anyone who leads:

operations, executive presence, leadership teams, operational effectiveness, process improvement, organizational excellence, business strategy, and general management.

In other words, someone who is not the CEO, but has the executive maturity required to manage them.

WHAT'S MY STORY?

Career Progression

- ↓ **News desk Intern**
- ↓ **Customer Service Agent**
- ↓ **Communications Manager**
- ↓ **PR/AR Manager**
- ↓ **Product Manager**
- ↓ **Business Manager**
- ↓ **Chief of Staff**
- ↓ **Director Business Services**
- ↓ **Chief of Staff**
- ↓ **Business Owner**
- ↓ **Responsible AI Director**
- ↓ **Chief of Staff**

AND

Mother
Grandmother
Wife
Divorcee
Neurodiverse
Evangelist
Activist
Advocate

PLUS

Just comfortable being me!

I had dreams of being a star…

So, studied business communications?

Which led me into my passion of telling "the story."

Regardless of audience, regardless of motivation, there is a narrative behind everything that you do, want to get accomplished, or need to convince other people to believe in you. The Story.

TV WASN'T FINISHED WITH ME YET!

My story went from broadcast communications to corporate and business communications. This landed me at the center of public relations, analyst relations, executive communications, investor relations, public speaking, and so much more. I never heard of the Chief of Staff role until a presentation on stage had a hiring manager knocking at my door.

GOODBYE DON!

A JOB MUST BE RIGHT FOR THE EMPLOYER AND THE EMPLOYEE

Before finding my passion and calling to be a career Operations Executive and Chief of Staff, I wanted to build an empire!

This drive led me to participate on one of the hottest REALITY TV shows of the time.

I was the FIRST person to ever QUIT!

Little did I know what was in store for the man I quit on...

Goodbye! I wouldn't change a thing!

SO, I PACKED MY BAGS...

Left the drama behind...

And discovered, there is more drama in the Corporate world than any TV show could possibly compete against!

And THAT'S why the Chief of Staff role is so important! We help keep the drama to a minimal...
At least a person can try!

GET ON BOARD THE BANDWAGON

Although I consider myself one of the early pioneers in the Chief of Staff position, it has grown significantly in popularity for executives and organizations over the last several years. The position continues to evolve and expand. More and more organizations are recognizing the value of having a skilled and experienced Chief of Staff to help drive growth and success.

What started out as a niche position, mainly focused on supporting financial strategy for growing organizations, has transformed into a must-have position for any executive who wants to amplify the value of the CEO Office, gain greater clarity of purpose across the organization, and have a trusted resource to keep things moving forward. Some Board of Directors are even requiring CEOs to hire executive level Chiefs of Staff to help with the evolution of the business.

FREE SPACE

After getting a proof of the book... the layout was too tempting to not add space for coloring. I just couldn't help myself!

PATH TO IMPACT

PATHS TO OPERATIONS AND CHIEF OF STAFF SUCCESS

There is no one size fits all or crystal ball for becoming a Chief of Staff

The role is so ambiguous, that in order to be successful in it, the position takes someone who handles ambiguity and uncertainty with a smile, and can roll with whatever path, roadblock, or opportunity presents itself during the journey.

THERE IS NO SPECIFIC ROLE OR TITLE THAT GUARANTEES SUCCESS IN THE CHIEF OF STAFF POSITION

Instead of looking at titles, understand the skills and strengths of those who have been impactful in the role.

DO NOT PROCEED:
MUST-HAVE SKILLS

☑Leadership
☑Project Management
☑Strategic Thinking
☑Communications
☑Relationship Building
☑Problem Solving
☑Financial Acumen
☑Analytical Skills
☑Creative Genius

A Chief of Staff should be able to lead and inspire teams, both within and outside the organization. They should be able to provide guidance and support to team members to help them achieve their goals.

Good leadership requires a person with a high degree of emotional intelligence, including the ability to manage relationships effectively, empathize with others, and respond appropriately to emotional situations.

LEADERSHIP

Project Management

A Chief of Staff must have exceptional project management skill... or should I say, multi-project management skills.

You will always be required to manage multiple projects simultaneously, prioritize tasks, and ensure that deadlines are met.

Because projects span the entire organization and all stakeholders across and within it, you must have the capability to work effectively with various stakeholders, including executives, board members, employees, and external partners.

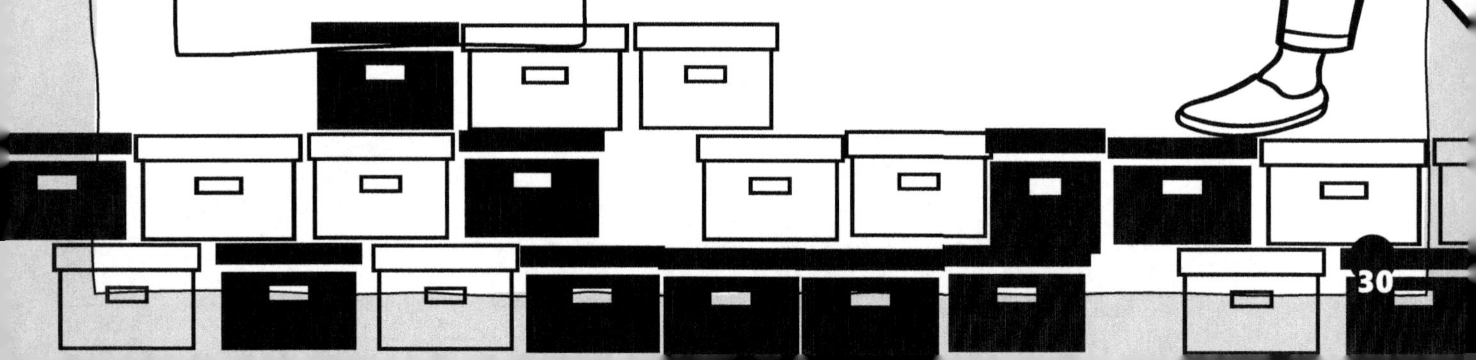

STRATEGIC THINKING

The ability to think strategically and see the big picture is essential for a Chief of Staff. They should be able to understand the organization's goals and help develop strategies to achieve them.

It is critical to have the skills necessary to adapt to changing circumstances and handle unexpected challenges with grace and resilience.

COMMUNICATIONS

From written and verbal communications, to perfecting the ability to negotiate, facilitate, and persuade, your communication skills will save you on many occasions.

You're not getting by without excellent communication skills. And this includes the full gamut of being able to understand your audience and connect with them.

RELATIONSHIP BUILDING

A Chief of Staff should be able to understand and manage their own emotions, as well as the emotions of others. This requires empathy, self-awareness, and the ability to build strong relationships with others.

Building strong relationships with a range of stakeholders, including the CEO, senior leadership team, and external partners is required if you want to be able to move programs forward.

A Chief of Staff should be able to analyze complex problems and develop innovative solutions. They need to be able to think critically and creatively to help the organization overcome challenges.

Your ability to adapt to changing circumstances and be flexible in how you approach problem solving, is a balancing act. Quickly thinking on your feet with the ability to adjust plans as necessary, helps keep team members on track with appropriate expectations set.

PROBLEM SOLVING

FINANCIAL ACUMEN

Even if like me, your favorite part of the role is NOT budget management, to really support a business end-to-end, you will need a good understanding of financial management and be able to use financial data to inform decision making.

By analyzing financial data, you obtain valuable insights into the company's operations and opportunities. This makes a significant difference in determining which strategies and initiatives to prioritize, as you realize the business can't do it all.

Strong analytical skills, is a must-have.

This includes the ability to analyze data, identify trends, and make data-driven decisions

Taking each task from a measured approach, thinking through complex scenarios and outcomes, will become an integral part of how you operate.

Keeping focused requires a natural ability to stay calm as you know you will figure it out. Regardless of how it works out. It WILL work out!

ANALYTICAL SKILLS

CREATIVE GENIUS

And, just as you thought that the role was focused on getting stuff done, you realize the level of creativity required to produce so many unique ideas, solutions, and just simply thinking outside of the box, is a natural talent and delight!

From events to motivating people in the organization, the Chief of Staff needs to be a consultant and coach to keep spirits high.

IS THAT ALL?

Wait, don't celebrate too quickly...

No, there's so many additional skills that come with a person being successful as a COS... learning and perfecting the basics will help you focus on many of the fundamentals required for the job.

Having the right mindset is a good place to start!

Personality, tolerance, confidence, and ability to translate, consolidate, predict and rescue! All play a significant role as well.

CHAPTER REFLECTIONS

Take a moment to reflect on what was covered in this chapter:

Anything new?
Anything surprising?
What aspects confirmed your own beliefs?

FREE SPACE

Doodling and coloring are actually relaxing ways to unlock your genius.

EXECUTIVE IN NAME ONLY?

"CHIEF" IN NAME ONLY?

So many reasons why the Chief of Staff title should be used sparingly. This is a unique role that requires a person who can design the box, build it, and fix the box if required!

Don't underestimate the knowledge and expertise required for the position, and label it, pay it, and acknowledge it accordingly.

There is so much to uncover which will help eliminate the "mystery" of the Chief of Staff function. Let go of your preconceived notions and have an open mind.

NOW, YOU MAY BE ASKING YOURSELF THE QUESTION

What exactly IS a Chief of Staff?

For those of us who have done the role, worked with the role, have seen individuals in the role, it might seem like this is obvious.

Someone who does it all and then some!

duh

DOING IT ALL IS JUST THE START

Many people mistake the Chief of Staff role as a support person, versus line of business owner.

They have it all wrong.

Owning programs and seeing the big picture, while enabling others to follow you on the journey IS one of the most important businesses of any organization.

WHAT IS IN A NAME?

The Chief of Staff role stretches across executive seniority positions, spanning CxO level to Director level.

It should never be positioned as a junior role, and never considered executive in "title" only.

The Chief of Staff role is a strategic position designed to support the CEO and senior leadership team in achieving organizational goals. While the Chief of Staff may assist with administrative tasks, their primary focus should be on developing and implementing strategies, managing special projects, and driving cross-functional collaboration.

WHAT EXACTLY IS...
A Chief of Staff

A support person, not an expert?

Well, only if you don't consider the ability to:

Prioritize and manage workstreams, budgets, headcount, events, internal processes, general complaints, executive egos, project and business management resources, deadlines, organizational change, Board of Directors, Controllers, roadmaps, people agendas, internal knowledge share, new hire onboarding, Executive offices, schedules, delegation, project completion, and generally, most things that keep the business ticking...

as requiring **EXPERTISE**, then yeah.

Oh, and forgot to mention

ALL at the same time!

PERFECTIONIST

I personally gave up on trying to be Perfect. I am grateful for the persona as it helped me at the beginning of my career. But to be a great leader and impactful COS, we realize we don't only expect perfection in ourselves, but a condition we are looking for in other people. That narrative must change to help people grow, find balance, and contribute their best self to the organization.

Perfection is always EXPECTED
No errors, they must be CORRECTED
Your persona purposely PROTECTED
The façade then gets PROJECTED
Hiding to pretend you're RESPECTED
Insecurities shouldn't be DETECTED
Bad thoughts would then be ERECTED
Will the real you just be REJECTED
Our perfection is so INEFFECTIVE

"IF I DON'T KNOW, I'LL FIND OUT!"

The COS should be ready and willing at any point to roll up their sleeves, jump in, and fix whatever the situation calls for. Coming across as strong, confident, "if I don't know I'll find out" attitude is the most well-known persona for the position. This is for good reason. The COS role is usually one with LOADS of responsibility, a HUGE amount of accountability, but in reality, very LITTLE authority.

With the appropriate boss, organizational culture, and leadership team, your AUTHORITY is amplified due to the magnitude of impact ALL employees, especially the CEO, require from you in this role.

WHAT EXACTLY DOES IT MEAN TO BE AN "EXECUTIVE?"

The "executive" is the person who has the ultimate weight of carrying the function and business forward, as both an internal and external representative for the organization.

Like the other "Chief" roles, the Chief of Staff should have the title and pay that goes along with all other executive roles in the company.

An executive function at any organization is typically the individuals who are responsible for steering the organization forward. Similar to the Finance Officer, Marketing Officer, People Officer, Diversity Officer, Product Officer, Legal Officer, Communications Officer, Operations Officer, Information Officer, or even Executive Officer, the term "CHIEF" that precedes the title bears the holder with the most senior level of expertise for that function.

CHAPTER REFLECTIONS

Take a moment to reflect on what was covered in this chapter:

Anything new?

Anything surprising?

What aspects confirmed your own beliefs?

FREE SPACE

Wouldn't be a workbook without having something challenging to work on!

Word Scramble

platerpsonie
rekrownetg
senohpilahster
shtdotioealymgoe
taygersr

mriabontensrgn
mtiaemennipelltnoi
napelemontdtav
ntilrspaoey
piuntptoryo

teecuxive
teksills
tnemotum
tnmaegamen
ytilitasopoh

eilibrtilay
elnivaalbu
enelclxece
lureictrutnaoc
mocenrperfa

aescriv
apnritsrehp
caytnali
crtieodr
ecnpxreeie

There is no rule saying I have to give you the answers in the back of the book... "If I don't know, I'll figure it out!" The COS way!

NEGOTIATING THE NON-NEGOTIABLES

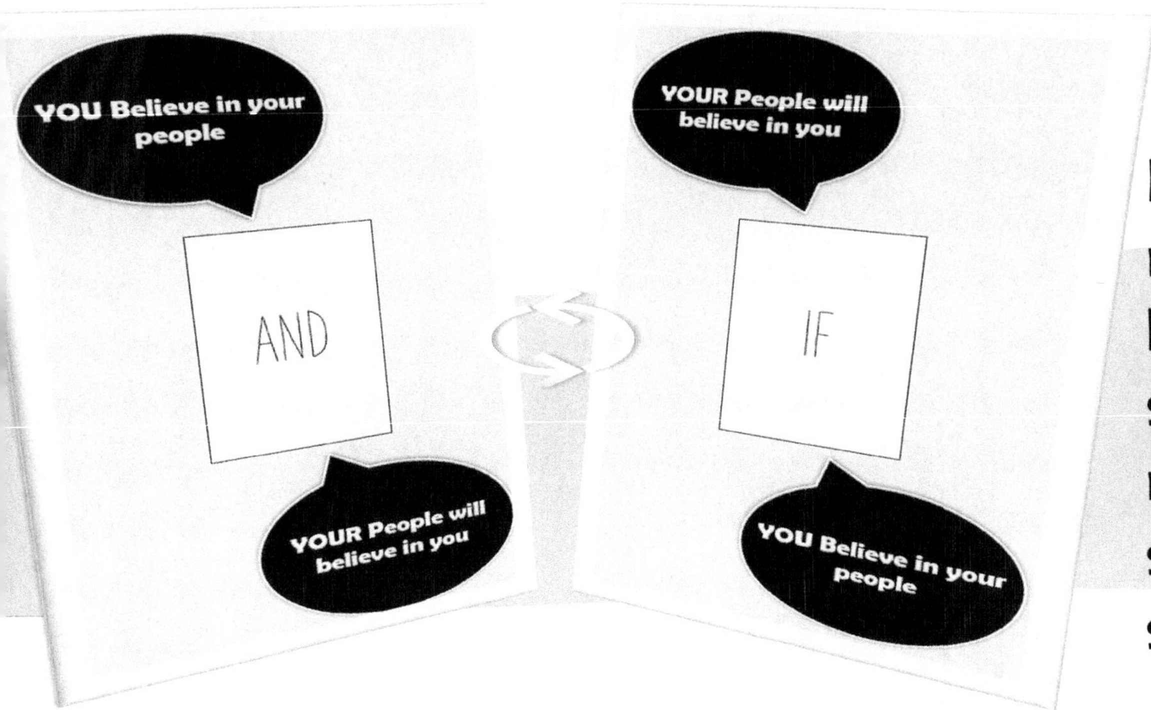

It doesn't matter how you spin it; the message is still the same!

Many organizations talk about "PEOPLE" being their greatest asset.

This is not just talk, but the reality of what actually underpins the organization's success.

The Chief of Staff role is the one who ties it all together. It is okay to negotiate your seat at the table, to identify agreements and expectations up front.

Know your worth and what you have contributed. Your success is not defined by the organization you work for, but their success most definitely is a result of your contributions!

I AM A CO-LEADER WITH THE SENIOR LEADERS OF THE ORGANIZATION

We need to respect one another and see each other as peers to understand there is no hierarchy when the doors are closed, and work needs to happen. There is no "rank order" when I need you to deliver what you committed, and I will hold you accountable to do just that. And there is no pecking order when my time is just as important as yours, and we need to find time to meet.

For the Chief of Staff role to successfully make impact:

WE WORK TOGETHER, AS A TEAM, WITH THE SAME GOALS IN MIND, AND WE MUST DO IT AS PARTNERS.

OTHER NON-NEGOTIABLES

DEFINED LINES OF AUTHORITY.

It is very important that the Chief of Staff roles, responsibilities, and lines of authority are clearly defined and known across the entire organization.

To ensure that the Chief of Staff can fulfill their responsibilities effectively, the CEO should delegate administrative tasks to other members of the team or support staff. This will allow the Chief of Staff to focus on high-level strategic initiatives that will drive the organization forward. Ultimately, the CEO and Chief of Staff should work collaboratively to ensure that their respective roles are clearly defined and aligned with the organization's goals.

Significant confusion and overlap in functions will become catastrophic in running the business. Overlaps in positions and decision-making cause territorialism and other unwanted, and unnecessary behavior.

Rethink the position, whether it is truly a COS role, or whether it is the right position for you, if it does not report accordingly.

The function of the Chief of Staff, especially as it relates to being a member of the leadership team, is ambiguous without adding extra layers of complication.

To be the trusted leader, coach, advisor, confidant, "get it done" person that the organization needs, there should be no layers between this role and the CEO.

UNDERSTANDING THAT I MIGHT NOT AGREE WITH YOU.

One of the most important responsibilities of a COS is to provide different viewpoints for consideration.

CEOs should not have clones of themselves.

Being a CEO is a lonely job. You never know who is telling you what you want to hear versus what you need to hear.

Have an opinion

Come with facts

Present with respect

Provide alternate perspectives

Pay on par with other executive functions.

It's complicated. I know. The Chief of Staff role takes care of so many things, from big to small. How do you possibly determine what level, what title, what seniority?

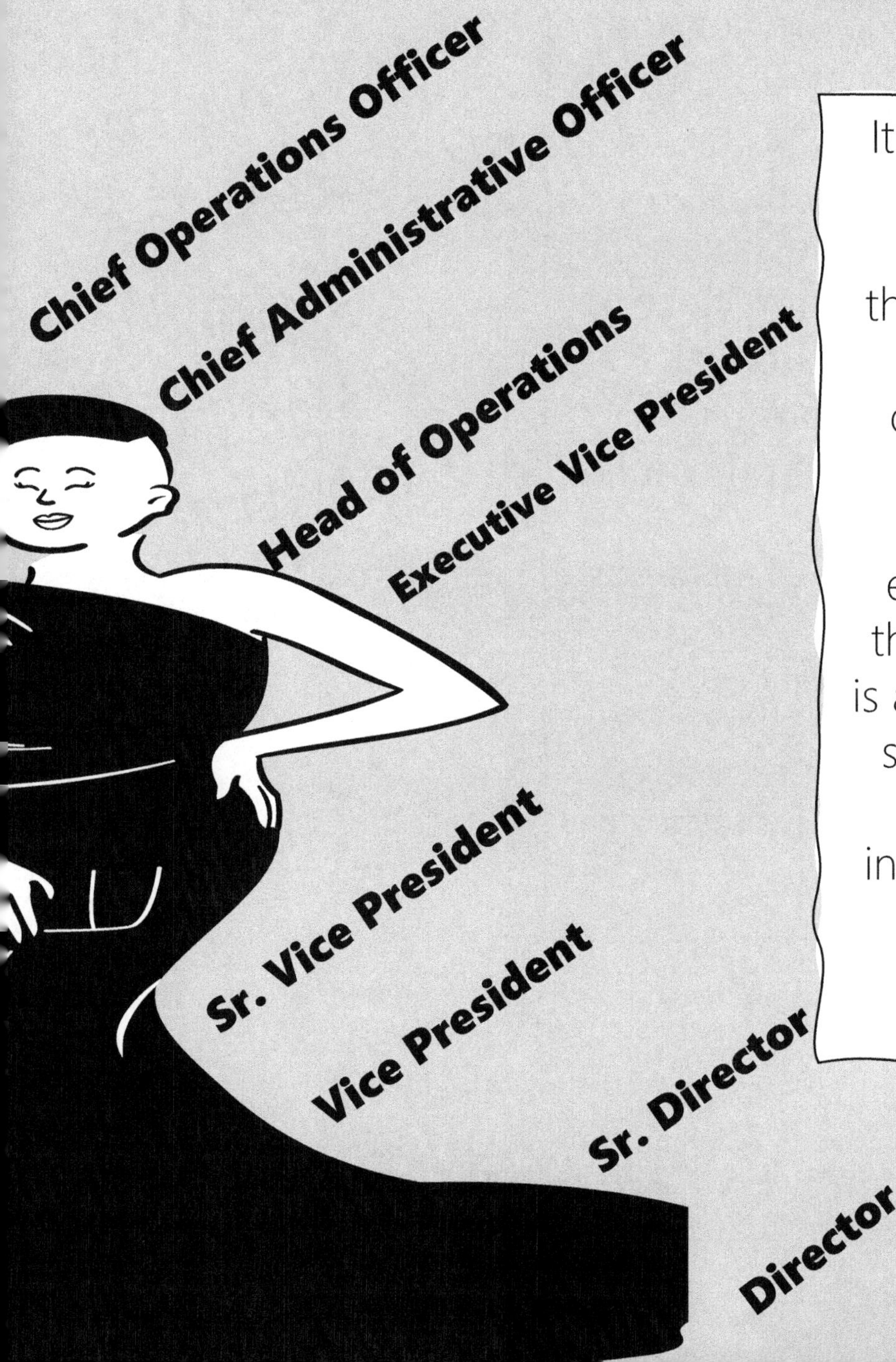

It's easy, remember this position holds the highest confidence to the CEO and should be respected and compensated as such. There is no one title that can encompass everything required of this role, but a title that is aligned with the other senior leaders that this role will need to interact with and direct, is the best place to start.

HC AND RESOURCES ARE IMPORTANT IF YOU WANT ME TO... "DO IT ALL."

Just like any business or function, you must spend money if you want to make money. If it wouldn't be expected that the marketing, finance, legal, human resources, or other operational businesses to function without staff, then it's probably not appropriate to understaff the Chief of Staff office.

Consider all that the COS is taking on, and plan resources accordingly. This might include an Executive Assistant who can ensure that the schedule and the myriad of responsibilities that will be delegated to you stay fantastically coordinated and balanced.

Depending on the business, EA support might be essential.

Our conversations do not need to begin with, *"I'm telling you this in confidence."*

That is already a given. Whatever we discuss, is between the two of us. Unless we explicitly acknowledge that the details are ready to be shared.

This goes for the CEO, to members of the leadership team, to employees who will use you as a sounding board for ideas and feedback. Confidence and discretion, is a non-negotiable must-have in the role.

I ATTEND ALL MEETINGS

...and events as a member of leadership.

It is difficult to lead the most senior people in the organization without authority. The authority is "assumed" based on the agreement that the Chief of Staff has with the CEO.

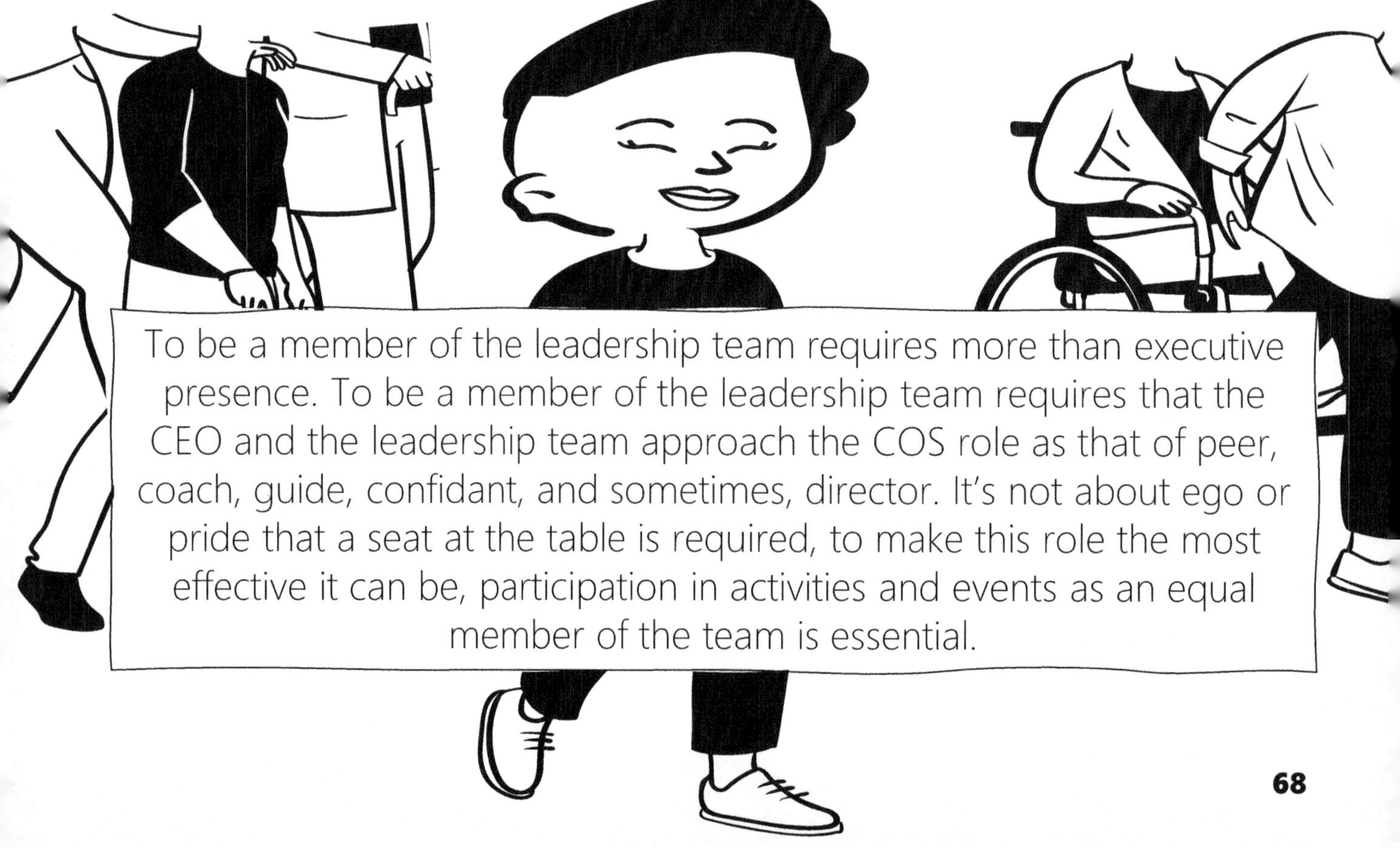

To be a member of the leadership team requires more than executive presence. To be a member of the leadership team requires that the CEO and the leadership team approach the COS role as that of peer, coach, guide, confidant, and sometimes, director. It's not about ego or pride that a seat at the table is required, to make this role the most effective it can be, participation in activities and events as an equal member of the team is essential.

Not to be overruled without discussion.

One of the most important things to remember is that the Chief of Staff is here to carry out the responsibilities, duties, and requirements of the CEO. The only reason the position exists is to be an extra set of hands, ears, eyes, and brain for the CEO, and to operate at scale, enabling the CEO to focus on parts of the business she prioritizes.

Establish rules of partnership up front. As a COS, you are often working on behalf of the CEO, so being able to understand and predict how that person will run the business is important. If you get it wrong, fess up to it, nothing wrong with that. But, set clear boundaries up front of how to deal with inaccurate interpretations, rather than figuring this out in front of employees. This is yet another interaction that can either strengthen the COS role, or cause others to reject it.

There are "Non-Negotiables" on both sides.

Don't settle on requirements needed to ensure the job can have the most impact, and enable the person in it to be as successful as possible.

With anything we want in life, we set boundaries on what is acceptable and what is not. The same should go for any position or role that you are considering. Whether you're looking to get hired for the job, or you're the one looking for someone to hire, you should have a very clear idea of what is "nice to" versus "must" HAVE.

Trying to negotiate important resources and authority can be very difficult after-the-fact. Be up front about your needs. If this one is not a good match, that means there is something even better waiting for you.

CHAPTER REFLECTIONS

Take a moment to reflect on what was covered in this chapter:

Anything new?
Anything surprising?
What aspects confirmed your own beliefs?

MORE FREE SPACE

THIS OR THAT?

CHOICES IN THE COS WORLD

There is a difference, but many people still mistake these roles as the same.

THERE ARE SWIM LANES

Many people do not realize there is a distinct difference between the Chief of Staff function and that of other supporting, administrative, and operational roles.

In order for people to stay in their swim lanes, those lanes (i.e., duties, areas of authority, priorities, ultimate point of impact) need to be defined and clearly understood by all. Partnership is a key part of each of these positions, and providing an opportunity to bring projects together creates a mutual trust and understanding, that goes a long way towards creating a healthy organizational environment.

So, what roles get confused with the position of Chief of Staff?

Here are just a few:

And although there is significant aspects of each of these functions in the Chief of Staff role, and a COS should be proficient in understanding each of the positions in depth, a COS is not any of these things.

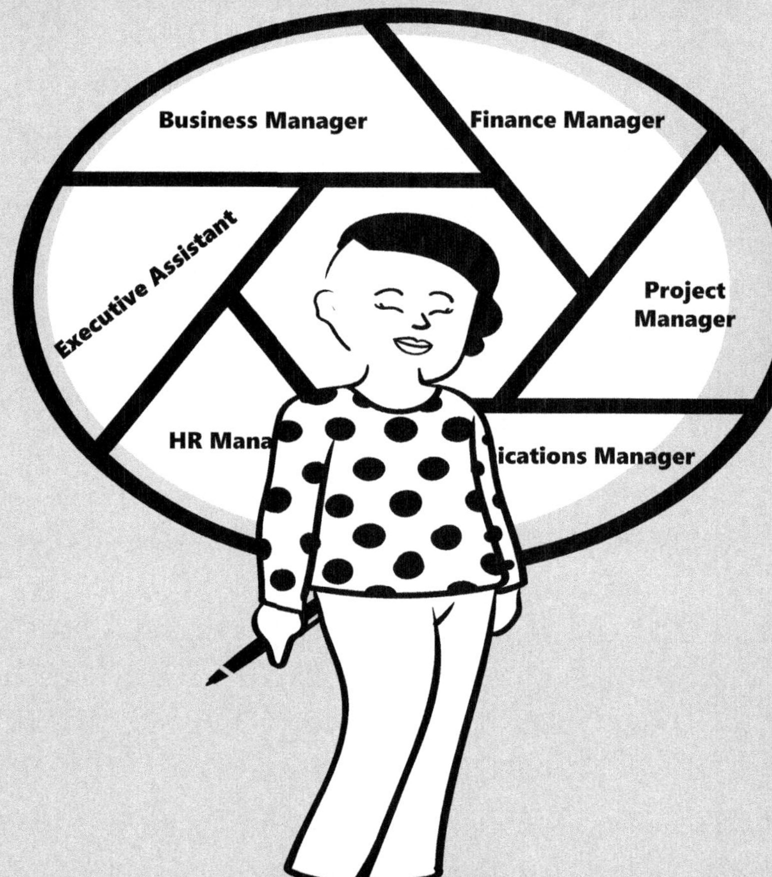

There is a clear set of responsibilities where the COS will partner with these roles, but important to not be confused with them.

WHAT CAUSES THE CONFUSION?

For most of the other operational and admirative functions, people do not "mistake" the COS for those roles as much as getting confused between the COS role and that of a

Business Manager, Executive Assistant, or Project Manager.

The primary reason for the confusion is lack of clarity on the seniority and "**swim lanes**" for the COS compared to these specific roles.

Setting clear lines of communication with regular check-ins, will greatly limit future conflict that can arise through role ambiguity.

HELP WANTED:

Business Manager

COS to BM Comparison

You can actually think of the Business Manager role as a precursor to the Chief of Staff function. The primary difference between the two is that the COS is a peer to the Senior Leadership team, creates the strategy and vision for operations, whereas the BM is primarily responsible for executing on all aspects of the operational strategy. When CEO level, Business Managers usually report to the COS, or more junior execs might have a BM act as a COS. Regardless it is a dynamic partnership that helps execute on all fronts!

Core Function

- Develop and implement business plans and strategies that align with the organization's goals and objectives
- Manage budgets and financial resources, including forecasting and reporting
- Collaborate with various teams to identify and implement process improvements and operational efficiencies
- Oversee project management activities and ensure that projects are completed on time, within scope, and within budget

HELP WANTED:

Executive Assistant

COS to EA Comparison

The Chief of Staff is responsible for overseeing the operations of the entire business or organization. The Executive Assistant (EA) is responsible for owning the productivity of the CEO specifically. The two roles must partner extensively to ensure time management and when an opportunity is an effective use of the CEO time, compared to when delegating to others in the organization is more appropriate.

Core Function

- Manage the CEO or top executive's calendar, scheduling meetings and appointments as needed
- Make travel arrangements, including booking flights, hotels, and rental cars
- Prepare and organize documents, presentations, and other materials as needed
- Manage correspondence, including screening and responding to emails and phone calls

HELP WANTED:

Project Manager

COS to PjM Comparison

Having a well-organized project manager is essential for success of the business as well as that of the Chief of Staff. The PjM role is one that is a crucial resource to help drive organizational productivity. The roles really are very different positions with entirely different objectives. One oversees projects and programs from inception to completion, then moves on to the next project. The COS runs and end-to-end business focusing on long-term strategy and success of the organization holistically.

Core Function

- Develop project plans, including timelines, budgets, and resource requirements
- Work closely with the project team to ensure that all project deliverables are completed on time, within budget, and to the required quality standards
- Identify and manage project risks, and develop contingency plans as needed
- Communicate regularly with stakeholders, including project team members, executives, and external partners or vendors
- Develop and maintain project documentation, including project plans, status reports, and other relevant materials
- Continually monitor project progress, and adjust plans and resources as needed to ensure successful project completion

AND WHAT ABOUT THE OTHER POSITIONS?

Confusion, overlap, and duplication in these roles generally happen as a result of unclear communications. The COS role is none of these (not even close!). However, these functions are critical in running an effective business. Therefore, many of the initiatives overseen by the COS requires close partnership with these functions in order to implement and cascade business priorities both internally and externally.

HR Manager

Chief Operating Office

Finance Manager

Communications Manager

... And So Many More!

WHICH ARE YOU AND WHAT IS THE DIFFERENCE?

Career vs. Rotational

WHICH ARE YOU AND WHAT IS THE DIFFERENCE?

Rotational

- **DURATION**

  18-24months, depending on seniority, business need, and stress tolerance.

- **PURPOSE**

  Either to drive greatly needed change, or to learn significant executive back-office skills in the FastTrack for career advancement.

- **EXPERTISE**

  Specified Line of Business Leader. Finance. Revenue growth. Organizational Change. Community builder.

- **COMPLAINT**

  Is my time over already, I still have so much more to do!

WHICH ARE YOU AND WHAT IS THE DIFFERENCE?

Career

- **DURATION**

We have you for the rest of your life!

- **PURPOSE**

Become the trusted shoulder, guide, and confidant to the CEO to help transform the business or keep a transformational organization innovative.

- **EXPERTISE**

Change agent. Executive Coach. Bringing structure to chaos. Making the impossible possible. Operating on behalf of others. Putting out fires. Living without ego.

- **COMPLAINT**

"To-do" lists that never get done!

THE WORK IS PRETTY MUCH THE SAME

Regardless of the amount of time a person plans to spend in the COS role, there is rigor to drive in the way the business operates. Whether it's in how you reach and engage employees, to how you demonstrate success to the Board of Directors, or even getting your finances in order, the role is at the center of it all.

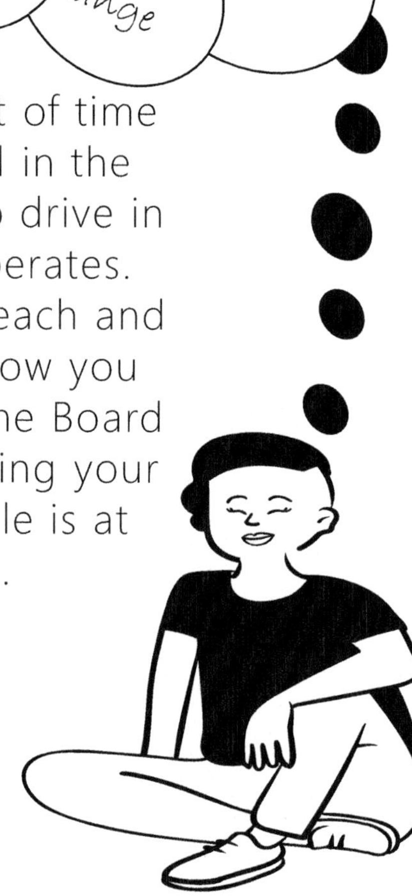

From planning what needs to get done, to making sure it happens. Either COS role type should be able to take the organization to the next level.

BOTTOM LINE

A career Chief of Staff is a long-term position in which the individual is focused on providing ongoing support to the CEO or other senior executives. They typically have extensive experience in the organization and are seen as a trusted advisor and strategic partner to the leadership team. While career Chief of Staff positions may have different titles and levels of seniority depending on the organization, the focus is on providing consistent support over a longer period.

A rotational Chief of Staff is a temporary position in which an individual is selected to serve as the Chief of Staff for a limited period, before rotating out of the position to allow for fresh perspectives and new ideas. This approach is often used in organizations that value diversity of thought and want to ensure that their Chief of Staff role does not become stagnant or too closely associated with a particular individual.

There is no right or wrong direction an organization can choose when determining which type of Chief of Staff is right for them. Regardless of whether Career or Rotational, you are sure to get a high-performing employee who has strong foundational expertise in multi-business and functional capability. They are adaptable, and always open for learning something new, or trying things a different way.

SECTION REFLECTIONS

Do you have a preference? Which resonates best with you:

CAREER or ROTATIONAL?

Although you may not get to determine this wholly, it's important to understand your own personal preferences.

SHADOW

Shadow SHADOW OR EXTENSION EXT.

Do you know the difference?

At the end of the day, the choice will most likely not be yours, but wholly dependent on how the organization has historically hired and positioned the Chief of Staff function,

SHADOW Shadow SHADOW OR EXTENSION EXT.

The decision usually comes from the CEO if a preference exists.

There are some Chief of Staff roles that are expected to participate in almost every meeting, event, and trip that the CEO engages. These are typically called SHADOW Chiefs of Staff.

There are commitments and actions coming out of most of these sessions, and it's important to have someone there on the other end to be the proactive "Catcher" to ensure that the necessary next steps take place. Additionally, these types of COS help facilitate and keep the meetings on track, and organized for efficiency so less advanced prep work is needed by the CEO.

Some executives prefer the Chief of Staff to manage a completely different set of business initiatives and priorities. They are their own "Catcher" or expect other employees in each meeting to take on that role.

For EXTENSION Chiefs of Staff, you are typically the delegate over other programs, representing the CEO, and you provide status updates to the CEO, and vice versa so you each are informed and knowledgeable about the full extent of activities occurring in the Office of the CEO.

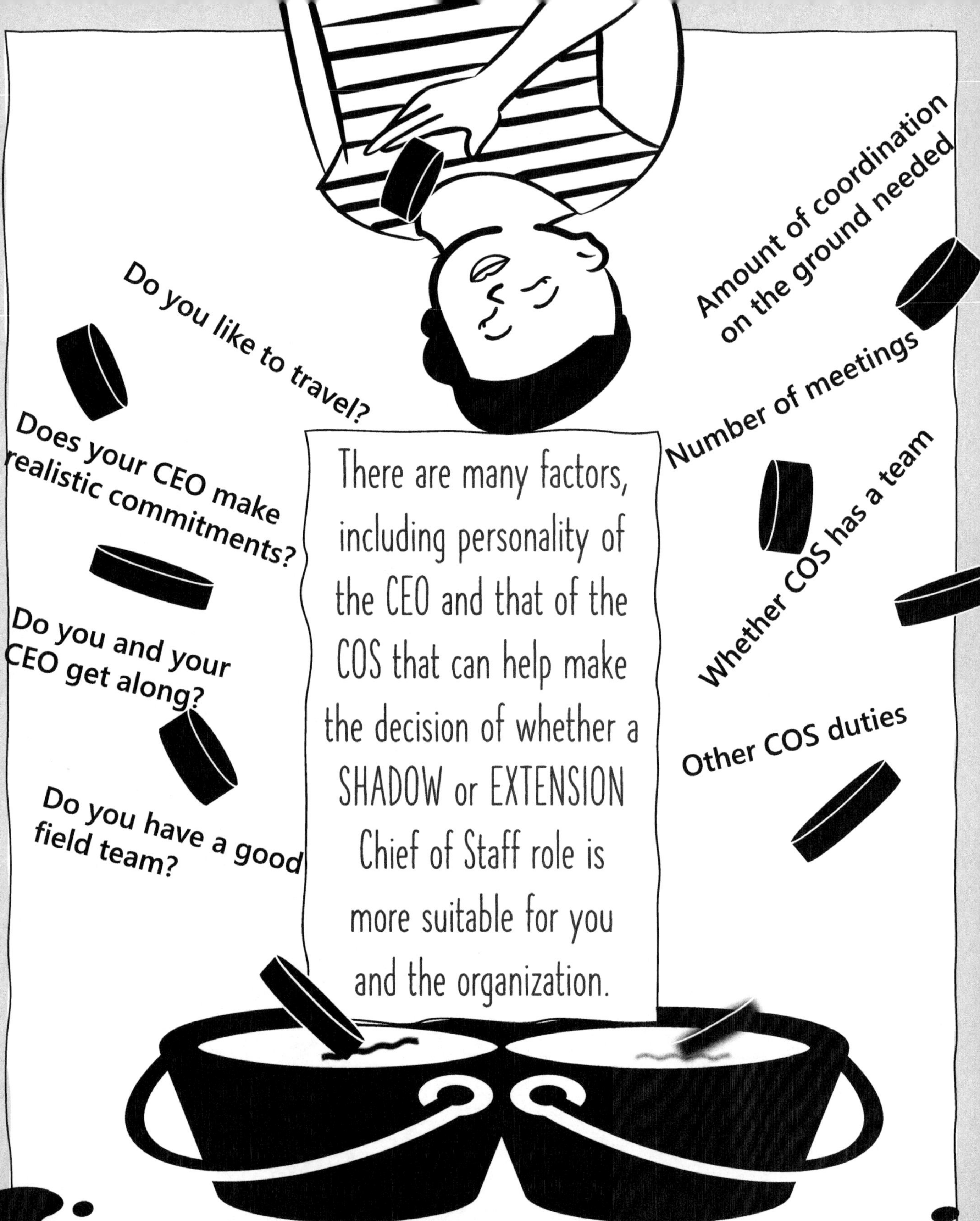

Many factors help determine if a CEO or position is the right one for you.

SO MANY DECISIONS TO MAKE... BUT HOW DO YOU DECIDE?

Yes, it's very true that the Chief of Staff function comes with a lot of decision-making responsibility. Regardless of whether Shadow or Extension, the role is designed to push the business forward and keep allocated areas of responsibility on track.

Luckily, this is actually one of those decisions you don't need to spend a lot of time on, as many factors will ultimately determine which type of COS is best for the business.

You should know your preferences though!

SECTION REFLECTIONS

Do you have a preference? Which resonates best with you:

SHADOW or EXTENSION?

Although you may not get to determine this wholly, it's important to understand your own personal preferences.

CHAPTER REFLECTIONS

Take a moment to reflect on what was covered in this chapter:

Anything new?
Anything surprising?
What aspects confirmed your own beliefs?

PEEK INTO (SOME) ROLES & RESPONSIBILITIES

ROLES & RESPONSIBILITIES

...to name a few

Board of Directors
Confidant & Coach
Executive Communications
Industry Engagement
Internal Events & Morale
Key Performance Metrics
Leadership Team
OPEX Budget
People Performance
Rhythm of the Business
Strategy Reviews
Special Projects
Time Management

And yes, they sometimes drop!

"THE GIVEN"

These are the basics. What to expect of every COS regardless of background and expertise. How a COS may approach each of these areas, directly correlates to their background, areas of interest, size of team, and overall state of the business. Teams should expect that any COS come prepared to add the layer of structure and rigor through these "GIVEN" workstreams.

RHYTHM OF THE BUSINESS

A rhythm of the business (ROB) or rhythm of operations, is a carefully constructed framework is built based on all things that will help run the business and make each individual employee understand their role in the organization's success.

The pieces in the framework can be seemingly unrelated, but the COS is a master at connecting the dots and organizing a strategy that enables all work and activities to co-exist in a predictable, repeatable manner.

This results in a fundamentally improved employee experience, where time is spent proactively on well-coordinated activities, to make room for the fires that need to be put out when those arise. This strategy connects the leaders to each line of business, the Board of Directors, to the future opportunities, and the employees to career growth and satisfaction.

You've heard the term. You know the drill. It's a fancy word for a set of meetings and business calendar... Right?

WRONG!

From the date of the meeting, to the agenda, workback schedule, presentation, content contributors, speakers, time allocations, notes, action items, follow-up, closure, report-out to stakeholders and employees...

You've got one HECK of a job on your hands!

The entire leadership team members have their own businesses to run in addition to the content, narrative, updates, numbers, more corrections, and final feedback needed from them.

Managing the Board of Directors engagement takes significant executive perception and maturity. What did we report at the last Board meeting, what expectations did we set for this meeting, and what feedback was given from the Board.

As one of the most critical responsibilities of your role, your job is to keep everyone calm, cool, and collected, confident, on task, and on schedule. You are the movie director, screenplay writer, producer, and actress, with lines in every scene. This is one starring role that will surely win best performance.

BOARD OF DIRECTORS MEETINGS

LEADERSHIP TEAM EXCELLENCE

As a Chief of Staff, the time the leadership team spends together, is probably your responsibility.

How often do we need to meet?

What do we need to discuss?

When do we make decisions vs. being informed only?

Who do we need to hear from?

There is a lot of work and planning to ensure the time spent together with the leadership team is productive, engaging, builds community, and ensures you are addressing leaders, people, and organizational concerns.

These meetings could manifest in weekly, bi-weekly, or monthly sessions. In addition to the frequency needed to take care of regular ROB activities, you will also schedule quarterly, semi-annual, or annual leadership team offsites as well. These offsites offer an opportunity to strategically plan, partner, and reframe how you innovate and successfully move the organization forward. Not to mention, there is always an opportunity for the leadership team to do constructive fun and engaging activities to get to know one another and build trusting relationships.

Remember this...

YOU ARE PART OF THE LEADERSHIP TEAM

KEY PERFORMANCE METRICS

Key Performance Indicators (KPIs)
Objectives and Key Results (OKRs)
or just simply, get your SH*T together!

Whatever the name, the leaders, managers, employees, and Board of Directors, need to understand what the company intends to accomplish and how the organization can measure success.

By working closely with the CEO and other key stakeholders, the Chief of Staff can help create effective OKRs that align with the organization's overall strategic goals, improve performance, and drive success.

Having aligned OKRs ensures that everyone is clear on priorities, and has a deep understanding of how their work contributes to delivering the mission, vision and strategy of the organization.

The Executive Assistant Partnership, is the most important one to establish.

TIME MANAGEMENT

How the CEO makes the most effective and efficient use of her time, is the responsibility of you, as Chief of Staff, and the Executive Assistant. The EA owns the calendar, owns the schedule, and is wholly responsible for protecting the CEOs time with meetings and activities that are essential and supports the overall role the CEO does for the organization.

As the Chief of Staff, your responsibility is to partner with the EA and determine priority of requests, with the business need and operational cadence. There are times when you must assess whether the CEO is the appropriate person for the meeting, or if one of her direct reports, or another person in the organization, should own the meeting instead.

Additionally, as you may be in several meetings with the CEO, you can foreshadow important meetings that need to be held, and get those set up in advance, based on priorities discussed. The CEO's schedule is only filled with the most critical items that the CEO, EA, and COS triage, will help you focus your CEO's time where they are needed most.

THE EXPECTED

In addition to the operational duties to help keep chaos down to a minimum, the COS role has become synonymous with internal communications and executive engagement.

Oftentimes the COS is the one person who has regular touch-points with the CEO and knows their schedule. As the delegate, facilitator, and gatekeeper of all things important, the COS can often get involved in directing activities to ensure all preparation has been performed to the required standard.

STRATEGY REVIEWS

Walking the organization through the development of OKRs, KPIs, and other measures that you and the leadership team will use to track progress against company priorities is just the start.

You must now establish a weekly, monthly, quarterly, and annual cadence that will help you perform regular check-ins. This ensures established priorities continue to be the right ones, and that when the end of the year approaches, there are no surprises as to whether organizational goals were obtained or not.

There will most likely be several types of strategy review sessions to cover various aspects of the business. These reviews may come in the form of Product Reviews, Monthly Business Reviews, Finance Reviews, Quarterly Business Reviews, Strategy Planning Sessions, People Reviews, and more. Regardless of what you call them, these sessions help facilitate deep-dive conversations that hold a mirror to the business in a way that is helpful and course-correcting.

INTERNAL EVENTS & EMPLOYEE MORALE

Nurturing a culture embodied in organizational values and principles requires a CEO who brings employees together and motivates teams to do their best work.

Having a strong relationship with the Chief Human Resources Officer and each member of the Senior Leadership team will help ensure that the activities and events meet the need in helping each employee feel part of the bigger team.

The Chief of Staff is often responsible for strategizing internal activities and events that align with the ROB, ensure all employees across the organization are kept updated on priorities and progress against them, and to ensure that the CEO's time in front of employees is maximized and effective.

OPEX BUDGET

The Chief of Staff will often work closely with the finance team to collaborate on budget planning and financial analysis, ensuring that the company's finances are in order and that resources are being allocated effectively. Combining operating revenue and financial acumen, provide important insights into the organization's operations and priorities, which help inform financial decision-making.

Having a strong partnership with the organization's CFO and finance team provides invaluable insights into the company's operations and opportunities for improvement. Those insights are then analyzed to develop many of the strategies and initiatives the COS creates in the role.

Prioritization of funds, supported by a healthy balance of expenses ... equals need and opportunity beautifully coexisting.

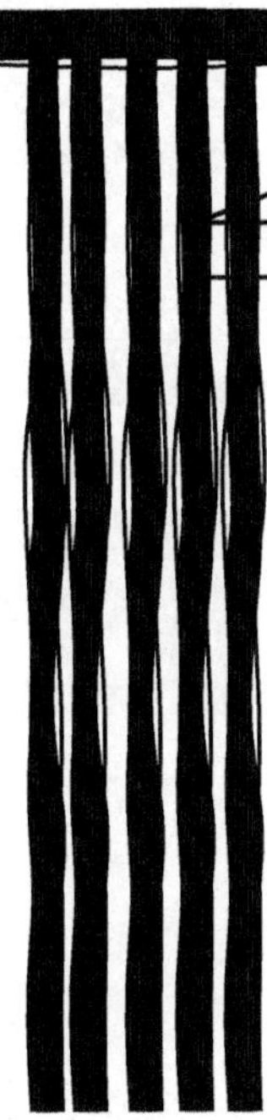

EXECUTIVE COMMUNICATIONS

Whether writing speeches, preparing presentations, drafting strategy memos, or contributing a quote, executives find themselves in numerous circumstances where what they say (or write), and how they say it, can have major impacts to the organization, partners, customers, and even motivating internal teams and employees.

Even if you have a person, department, or group of people specifically responsible for the CEO's communications strategy, the COS will generally partner with those individuals. The COS is in the perfect position to ensure the content of messages reflect the latest business priorities, and company direction. Also, through the Office of the CEO, the ability to help orchestrate what prep time, rehearsals, or other meaningful aspects of the presentation or event, is another focus of the COS role.

The CEO "Brand" is critical both internally and externally!

INDUSTRY ENGAGEMENTS

Depending on the type of organization you're in, there may be different types of engagements an executive will be involved in. This could include customer meetings, sales meetings, partner meetings, roundtables, and more.

Engagements are a great way to get out of the office and get a real sense of what's happening in application. These experiences are a great way to not only drive awareness and loyalty to your organization's brand, but also a great way to hear and learn from the people in the industry that matter to you the most.

The Chief of Staff must make sure that these meetings, events, and sessions are carried out to perfection. This includes working with the account teams and customer organizations to develop mutually beneficial itineraries, to ensuring that the overall purpose of the meeting actually occurs during the conversation. From briefing templates, to prep calls, to steering the conversation as a participant in the meeting, and then following up to ensure everyone delivers on commitments, the COS play an integral part in making these engagements a valuable use of the CEO's time.

THE STRETCH

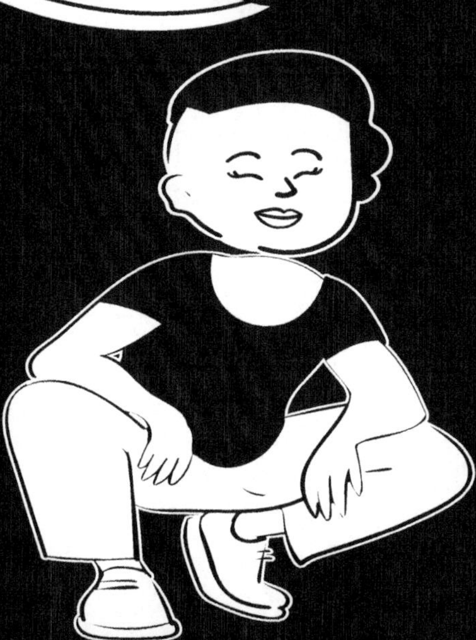

And, because there is no such thing as a comprehensive COS Job Description, there is a host of other responsibilities that can't be predicted. This need surfaces quickly in the role, and the COS is just the trusted and capable person to handle the job.

(what you thought the piece of paper you read with responsibilities on it was a definitive list of things you will manage? Ha ha)

PEOPLE PERFORMANCE

Partnering with the Chief Human Resources Officer and others in HR is essential for organizational operations and to ensure the greatest impact of all teams and functions.

TALENT MANAGEMENT and developing a comprehensive senior leadership strategy that includes recruitment, training, and prioritization.

SUCCESSION PLANNING collaboration to identify potential successors, assessing their readiness for the role, and creating a plan to develop their skills and experience.

ORGANIZATIONAL HEALTH measured through polling, feedback, and action plans to hold the Senior Leadership Team accountable for maintaining a culture aligned to company values.

ORGANIZATIONAL DEVELOPMENT required to assess the structure and analyze opportunities where changes can be made to improve efficiency and effectiveness.

EMPLOYEE ENGAGEMENT for creating a culture where employees feel valued and supported, and ensures employee concerns and feedback are understood by the Senior Leadership Team.

...are just a few examples

CONFIDANT & COACH

How can the COS manage so many aspects of the business without also being confidant and coach?

You might think that this should be included in THE GIVEN section.

Isn't the entire purpose of a COS to be the trusted advisor to the CEO...

This is not a given as there are many factors, primarily relationship and trust between the Chief of Staff and CEO that enables the COS to act in the capacity as confidant and coach.

This should be the ultimate goal of the relationship, if the COS is truly to provide the greatest amount of impact to the organization.

SPECIAL PROJECTS

You will very seldomly see a Chief of Staff role posted without the mysterious:

"...and special projects as assigned"

noted at the end of any job description and set of responsibilities for the COS function.

What does this even mean?

It means exactly that.

The list of possible projects and programs that might be "assigned" is endless and depends on the organization, the industry, the capabilities of the leadership team and their team members, the specific areas of expertise the COS brings into the position, and overall, the level of trust that the COS and CEO have established that the COS can just, "get it done."

And what are examples of special projects?

SPECIAL PROJECTS

Whenever anything, in any function, needing just about any area of expertise arises... the COS role is at the top of the list for taking it on. If a project or program requires the CEO's attention, the COS is usually delegated to manage it on their behalf.

Change Management
Help an organization navigate through periods of change, such as mergers and acquisitions, organizational restructuring, or the implementation of new systems and processes.

Training and Development Provide training and development programs to help employees build the skills and knowledge they need to achieve their goals and contribute to the success of the organization.

Risk Management
Identify and manage risks, ensuring that it is well-prepared to deal with potential threats and challenges.

Communications Strategy
On point to ensure key messages are delivered effectively to stakeholders and the wider public.

Policy Development
Support the development of policies and procedures that are aligned with organizational goals and objectives.

FREE SPACE

CHAPTER REFLECTIONS

Take a moment to reflect on what was covered in this chapter:

Anything new?
Anything surprising?
What aspects confirmed your own beliefs?

WHAT WE ARE NOT

So, now you've realized the COS role is probably a lot more complex and integral to running the organization than you imagined.

How can one person wear so many hats?

It's true, the Chief of Staff must take on many roles across the organization, and step in and step up at any time the need calls for it.

In that type of situation, this is a function that can also be misconstrued and taken advantage of. That is why it's important to remember the COS is many things, but there are also things that the function is not.

WHAT WE... ARE NOT

- An easy way to add diversity to your leadership team
- The person responsible for delivering the hard messages because you cannot
- Your personal assistant, or a title used to promote your EA
- Leadership team meeting note taker and agenda chaser
- The Boss, Project Manager, Business Manager, or Administrative Assistant
- A replica of the exec, or someone who tells you what you want to hear

AN EASY WAY TO ADD DIVERSITY TO YOUR LEADERSHIP TEAM

"That's ridiculous, an organization would never do that!"

YOU'D BE SURPRISED!

Having a diverse leadership team can help an organization better understand and meet the needs of a diverse customer base, leading to greater success and growth. By valuing and prioritizing diversity throughout the entire organization, you create a culture of inclusivity and innovation.

A diverse team brings different perspectives and experiences to the table, which can lead to better decision-making and a more inclusive work environment.

While having a diverse leadership team is important, it is equally important to have diversity throughout the entire leadership team and not just in roles that can be assumed to be support positions. The Chief of Staff role is often the lowest paid position of the senior leadership, which adds to it often being the simplest choice to achieve diversity goals.

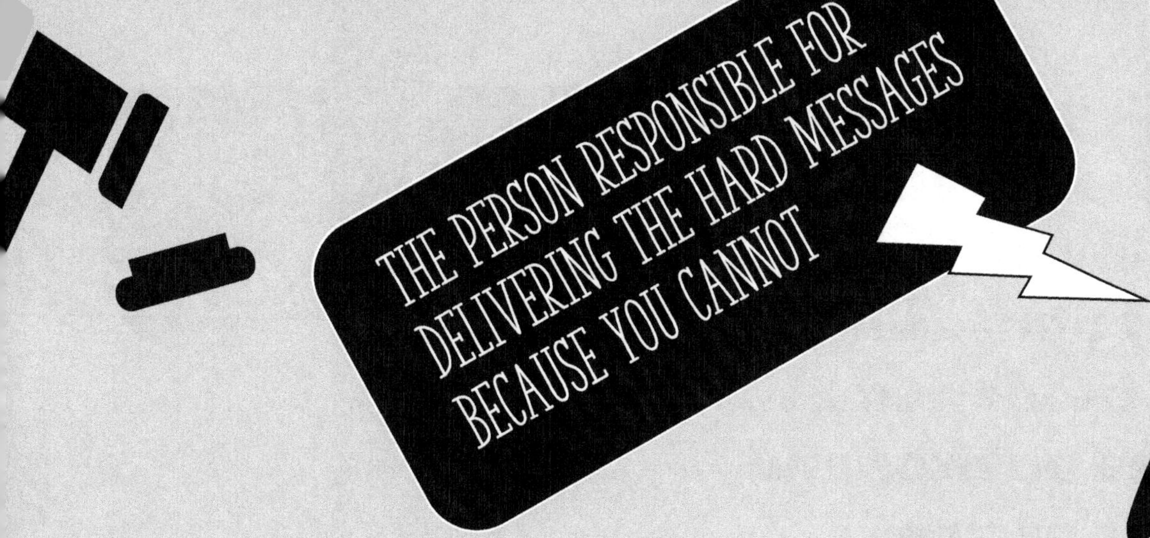

While the Chief of Staff can act as a trusted advisor to the CEO, it is important that the CEO is also involved in delivering bad news to the organization. This is because the CEO is ultimately responsible for the success or failure of the organization and needs to be seen as taking responsibility for any difficult decisions that need to be made.

If the Chief of Staff is always delivering the bad news, it can create a perception that the CEO is disconnected from the organization or is not willing to make tough decisions. This can erode trust in the CEO and ultimately harm the organization's culture and performance.

It is important for the CEO to take an active role in delivering difficult news, while working closely with the Chief of Staff to ensure that the communication is clear and consistent.

This will undermine the authority and credibility of the Chief of Staff, who should be viewed as a trusted advisor and strategic partner.

Using the Chief of Staff as a personal assistant can be detrimental to the organization's success. It can limit the Chief of Staff's ability to provide strategic support and may create a perception that the CEO is not capable of managing their workload effectively.

The Chief of Staff role is a strategic position designed to partner with the CEO and senior leadership team in achieving organizational goals. While the Chief of Staff may assist with administrative tasks, their primary focus should be on developing and implementing strategies, managing special projects, and driving cross-functional collaboration.

Pay your EA what they're worth as it is a senior function to be respected!

LEADERSHIP TEAM MEETING NOTE TAKER AND AGENDA CHASER

If it has to be chased, it's probably not worth catching.

As the key advisor to the CEO and liaison between the CEO and senior leadership team, the Chief of Staff is responsible for ensuring that the leadership team meetings are productive, efficient, and effective. While the Chief of Staff plays a critical role in shaping the agenda and identifying the key issues to be discussed, it is important to recognize that this is not their sole responsibility.

The COS must strike a balance between guiding the agenda and allowing the other members of the leadership team to prioritize programs, projects, and employees to discuss and highlight.

Success of the leadership team depends on the active engagement and participation of all members.

THE BOSS, PROJECT MANAGER, BUSINESS MANAGER, OR ADMINISTRATIVE ASSISTANT

The Chief of Staff has its own job title and set of priority responsibilities. The role should not need to be combined or mistaken for something it's not.

While the Chief of Staff may act on behalf of the CEO and have a high level of authority and influence, they are not the boss, and it undermines the CEO title to position the COS as such.

The Chief of Staff function is also more strategic and holistic than most other administrative and operations roles and should focus less on the tactical and specifics of deliverables.

A REPLICA OF THE EXEC, OR SOMEONE WHO TELLS YOU WHAT YOU WANT TO HEAR

As a key member of the leadership team the Chief of Staff has a critical role in ensuring that the organization achieves its goals. One of the key responsibilities is to provide an alternative viewpoint to the CEO. This is important because it allows the CEO and other executives to make better decisions by considering a wider range of perspectives and potential outcomes.

If the Chief of Staff always agrees with the CEO, then there is a risk of "groupthink" and the CEO may miss out on valuable insights and feedback. By having an alternative viewpoint, the Chief of Staff can challenge assumptions, raise concerns, and provide a different perspective that may be essential to the success of the organization.

Besides, the CEO should appreciate you bringing your own voice and strategy, opinions, and ideas to the table.

SO MANY, MANY THINGS.

A good Chief of Staff will make the job look easy.

A good CEO knows that it's not.

The Chief of Staff role has so many hats to balance. From understanding the details of finance, to driving business strategy, dealing with employee relations and customer satisfaction, being timekeeper, bookkeeper, and referee. There are so many things that WE ARE, it's seriously important to remember what we are not.

CHAPTER REFLECTIONS

Take a moment to reflect on what was covered in this chapter:

Anything new?

Anything surprising?

What aspects confirmed your own beliefs?

NOT ALL THAT GLITTERS

...THE NOT SO GOOD PARTS

You've got to be kidding!
THERE ARE DOWNSIDES TO BEING A COS?!

Yup, that's right. With all the excitement of shifting responsibilities, tasks changing daily, short and long-term planning, and helping to shape the impact of the entire organization... what could possible be better than that?

There is typically one executive Chief of Staff in an organization. Like that of the CEO, the position can get lonely and feel you are always leading, and never getting the chance to be led. Mistakes come at a high price, and it often feels perfection is THE primary qualification that should have been included in the Job Description.

There are plenty of other reasons a person may stay far away from taking on the COS title.

1. LACK OF AUTONOMY:

You will often be seen as a REFLECTION of the CEO, rather than a leader of your own right. This may require you to get approval on many decisions that you are highly capable of making.

Regardless of which priorities you are driving or want to work on in preference to other activities, if the duty calls for it, you will be redirected to other activities the CEO deems more important. This can happen even if you deem the priority to be less critical. You have less control of your work items and may feel like you're stranded on a desert when your job preferences seem less meaningful.

This can be frustrating for someone who is accustomed to having more independence in how they function and select projects and programs they desire to work on.

2. HIGH STRESS:

The Chief of Staff role is incredibly demanding and high-stress, requiring you to juggle multiple responsibilities and manage complex projects with tight deadlines.

Burnout is an easy ending in the role for those who cannot learn to pace themselves. There is always something to get done and there is never enough time to do it all.

This is one of the reasons some people choose rotational COS positions, rather than taking the high-demanding role as a long-term career choice.

DID I MENTION HIGH-STRESS?

3. LACK OF CLEAR JOB DESCRIPTION:

Oftentimes, the CEO isn't even sure exactly what they want from the COS role.

The Chief of Staff role can vary widely from one organization to another, with different expectations and responsibilities.

This lack of clarity can make it difficult for someone to know what is expected of them in the role.

It can be very disappointing if a person in the position needs to define their responsibilities based on the job description. Use the JD as a guide, but it's not a good expectation to use the JD as a map as it will not set you up for success in the long-term.

4. LIMITED UPWARD MOBILITY:

Does the title "Chief of Staff" satisfy you enough to encompass your expertise and business acumen?

Will you want more?

Depending on the organization, there may be only one Chief of Staff position, and that role is the most senior operations executive function at the company.
Where do you go next?

You've seen the conditions of being CEO and maybe that's not a career direction for you.

Despite what others may think, you ARE a line of business owner and the programs you lead are significant.

You have developed the expertise as any other CxO in the leadership, but not necessarily getting the rewards to match.

5. POTENTIAL FOR BURNOUT:

It's difficult to find balance when you desire to ensure all things are running smoothly at all times.

Due to the high demands of the role, there is a risk of burnout for those in the Chief of Staff role. Well, sort of. There are no structured hours for your job. What needs to get done, you get it done... and you get it done when it needs to get done. You are expected to and should be okay with prioritizing long hours and heavy workloads when the time calls for it. Which requires a careful balance to recharge and energize during periods of less chaos.

6. DIFFICULT PERSONALITIES:

The Chief of Staff will have to work closely with difficult and demanding individuals, which can be stressful and challenging.

- Leading the most senior leaders in the company can be a massive undertaking.
- Handling situations where employees are frustrated, upset, and disappointed is a core job function.
- Stepping in for the CEO at times where customers, team members, and others prefer to meet with the CEO, takes delicate care.
- Facilitating outspoken experts, and keeping them to meeting and prioritized boundaries, is never fun.

Sometimes your role is simply being the sympathetic ear.

7. LACK OF RECOGNITION:

Because the Chief of Staff role often involves working behind the scenes, it can be difficult for the individual to receive recognition or credit for their contributions.

Additionally, your job is often to ghost write for the CEO and to prepare content and strategies on their behalf. Your ideas turn into their ideas.

A person needs to have very little ego or feel rewarded by public promotion, as this is not a significant focus of the CEO to give you that recognition.

That should be credit enough?

8. NEVER FINISH YOUR "TO DO" LIST:

No matter how short or long (in this role your list will be very, very long), there is always something to get done. Put that list on hold because there is always priorities and other unknowns popping up during the day.

Do you enjoy putting out fires?
Do you want to be the first person people come to when something unexpected happens?
Can you handle not having the answers, or even knowing where to look for them, with ease?

If you get through 50% of your day's to-do list, count yourself as one of the lucky ones. This should be an expected part of the role, and "planning your day" is simply a suggestion.

9. ALWAYS IN HIGH-DEMAND:

Whether your inbox is a never-ending influx of requests, feedback, open decisions that need to be made, or just general inquiries and clarification, you should never have a dull moment.

Hope you are good at multi-tasking!

People will look to you for answers when they either cannot communicate with the CEO or need guidance in advance of meeting with the CEO to ensure the content is what needs to be shared.

10. TIED TO AN EXECUTIVE:

The career trajectory and performance of the executive directly reflects on you and your future opportunities.

You've been lucky to have found the perfect CEO to work with and for. You have a voice, can speak for yourself, and comfortable representing the CEO where needed. But what happens if that person leaves, is forced out, or in general, just isn't doing the best job?

In each COS role, you are not only making a bet that the company will succeed, but the CEO behind it will as well.

Whatever credibility, trust, and relationship you've built in this partnership, get ready to start again.

HAVE YOU EVER HEARD OF A PERFECT JOB?

There may be no "perfect" job, but there could be a position that is perfect for "YOU!" ...and that's what matters.

There are ups and downs, pros and cons, the good and the bad, to any position or function. The Chief of Staff role is no different. There are many factors that make the "cons" of this job not worth it for some people. Then, there are many people who actually consider those same "cons" to be "pros!"

...now THAT is something to think about!

EYES OPEN

If you are new to having a Chief of Staff, or new to the function, it can oftentimes be beneficial to "test" it out first. Nothing wrong with that, and nothing wrong if it doesn't work out. Some people know this is the life for them. For others, there could be a mis-guided belief that it really is greener on the other side.

The point is to walk into any position "Eyes Open." As much as possible, try to make sure you know what you're getting into. If it's not right for the business, then don't do it. If it's not right for the potential Chief of Staff, then don't do it. The role is not for everyone, and that includes employees and CEOs.

CHAPTER REFLECTIONS

Take a moment to reflect on what was covered in this chapter:

Anything new?

Anything surprising?

What aspects confirmed your own beliefs?

CHEAT SHEET

OTHER HELPFUL HINTS AND TIPS

WHY SO MANY TERMS
... and what do they mean?

Acronyms and "corporate speak" are all used to create a shared understanding of methodologies, programs, and processes with others in a constructive manner. This is helpful as it enables teams to work quickly together without the need to pause and define strategies each step of the way. Instead, jot down the acronym and revisit it later until you create your own COS Cheat Sheet.

This glossary provides a range of key terms and concepts associated with the Chief of Staff role, from strategic planning and OKRs to project management, delegation, and change management. Understanding these terms and their associated concepts is essential for succeeding in the Chief of Staff role and driving organizational success.

HERE ARE A FEW...

Like everything else in business, acronyms, terms, and catch-phrases vary by organization and industry.

Chief of Staff (COS):
The senior executive who serves as the primary strategic advisor to the CEO and is responsible for ensuring the CEO's directives are carried out effectively throughout the organization.

Objectives and Key Results (OKRs):
A management framework used to set measurable goals and track progress towards achieving them. OKRs typically consist of a set of objectives and several key results that are used to measure progress towards achieving those objectives.

Key Performance Indicator (KPI):
A specific metric used to measure progress toward a particular goal or objective.

Standard Operating Procedure (SOP):
A document that outlines a set of standardized steps or procedures for completing a specific task or process. SOPs are designed to ensure consistency and quality in the execution of tasks and are often used in industries such as manufacturing, healthcare, and finance. SOPs can also be used in non-industrial settings, such as in business operations or project management, to establish consistency and efficiency in processes.

Performance Management:
The process of setting expectations, measuring performance, and providing feedback to employees in order to improve performance and achieve specific goals and objectives.

Change Management:
The process of planning, implementing, and managing change within an organization, usually in order to improve performance or adapt to new challenges or opportunities.

SWOT Analysis:
An analysis of an organization's strengths, weaknesses, opportunities, and threats.

Quality Control:
The process of ensuring that products or services meet established quality standards.

Strategic Planning:
The process of defining an organization's goals, objectives, and strategies for achieving them, usually over a multi-year period.

Leadership Development:
The process of developing the skills, knowledge, and attitudes necessary to lead others effectively, usually through a combination of formal training and on-the-job experience.

Too many definitions and NEED TO KNOW words to list, but you get the point.

REPOSITORY OF THE MOST USED TERMS:

If your organization doesn't have a library or repository of some type that can be a good reference for new employees as they onboard, this might be one of the "Special Projects" that you should take on.

Don't underestimate the unique culture of each organization with their own words and acronyms. They may feel like "industry standard" to you, but believe it or not, many in the same industry have never heard of those terms.

Example:

I was in a customer meet with a colleague. We were meeting with the CFO and Finance team of a major retailer. My colleague mentioned the term "CPM" a few times early in the meeting. I paused and asked the group if they were familiar with the term "CPM" or "Corporate Performance Management."

My colleague rolled his eyes as though it were a stupid question, and of course, everyone in finance was aware of the term.

To his surprise the CFO spoke up and said, no, he had not heard the term. We then had the opportunity to clarify what it meant and put context around the entire conversation.

Sometimes even the "dumb" question is the one that needs to be answered first.

THERE IS NO DICTIONARY FOR THE COS...

The ability to excel as a Chief of Staff requires integrity, stamina, flexibility, and passion. There is no dictionary. You must write your own dictionary of what is needed for the CEO and organization overall, and that is your ultimate focus to ensure impact.

Your work ethic and ability to adapt to ever-changing circumstances, are key elements to consider.

Desire to put in the effort to complete tasks at a high level of quality, even when faced with challenges or obstacles. This involves being reliable and punctual, taking initiative to tackle tasks without being prompted, and being willing to go above and beyond what is expected.

Ability to quickly pivot your focus and rework an approach that aligns with the new direction, including the ability to identify new opportunities that arise from the change and demonstrate flexibility in adjusting the timeline or resources to accommodate the new direction.

RECRUITING TIPS!

A true COS can get the basics in place, while learning the other areas that need short, mid, and long-term attention.

When it comes to the Chief of Staff function, you can easily find a person with all of the skills outlined in this booklet. The fundamentals are the most important. Would definitely start there. However, if you're looking for someone who can check the box on all of the work items and responsibilitiess that the CEO needs to get accomplished, you're off track.

What's more important than finding someone who has perfected all Responsibilities and Qualifications listed in the Job Description, is the actual relationship.

You can find the most qualified candidate, who can do the job with their eyes closed, but if the relationship between CEO and COS is not a healthy one, you have the wrong person for the job.

MEET IN PERSON: Face-to-face exposure helps both parties get a better sense of one another's personalities, energy, and style. It's not a guarantee, but it should be required!

INTERVIEWING TIPS!

TIP #1: Be Yourself!

You don't NEED this job... there are other positions out there than to take one that is not a good fit for you, where you are in your career, and the type of Chief of Staff you want to be or have become.

TIP #2: Be Yourself!

Use your stories; what you've accomplished, how you did it, and the impact that it created. Share about your family, your life, and other things that are important. These all contribute to the Leadership style you bring to the organization.

TIP #3: Be Yourself!

Your skills, background, experiences, and unique areas of expertise have gotten you to where you are, and have gotten you the interview. Showing up as authentically you, will help the recruiter, the leadership team, the CEO, and other stakeholders get a true sense of who you are and what you bring to the organization. Showing up as the perfect, role model COS that the team expects, will ultimately place you in a culture that might not be suitable or desirable.

Another Tip!
Get it in writing...
or at least write
it down!

A contract?
Mutual agreement?
Common understanding?

Yes. Something like that.

ESTABLISHING TRUST

I've said it before, but there is no understating the importance of building a relationship between the CEO and Chief of Staff.

Ultimately, this is the MOST important activity and set of mutual agreements the two of you have.

Preferred mode of contact:

- ❑ Call
- ❑ Text
- ❑ IM
- ❑ Email

Ghost writing preferences:

- ❑ Outline
- ❑ Full script
- ❑ No help
- ❑ Early draft

Leadership team engagement:

- ❑ Less 1:1 w/ CEO
- ❑ Ops tasks only
- ❑ Prep for meetings
- ❑ Trusted ear

DOES THIS RESONATE?

You're a leader... and a follower.
A person who knows how to get the party started, and someone who knows when to let others steal the dance floor.

You keep calm even when you're scared. While telling people the truth about how scared you really are.

You're someone who is likeable, but never known to be a pushover. A person who can listen empathetically, and one who takes no excuses.

You're someone people might not want to be, while they're full of admiration for you at the same time.
A fighter, and someone who knows how to turn the other cheek.

You see "possible" where others see "impossible." And a solution when others only see chaos.

You don't know how this will end up.
...but you know it will work out in the end.

CHAPTER REFLECTIONS

Take a moment to reflect on what was covered in this chapter:

Anything new?

Anything surprising?

What aspects confirmed your own beliefs?

THE END?

THIS IS YOU

This is a SERIOUS book, about a SERIOUS role, with a set of SERIOUS responsibilities, for a person who probably takes themselves a little too SERIOUSLY!

Now that we have gotten that out of the way. Take a moment to reflect on whether you saw yourself in any of the scenes depicted in the book.

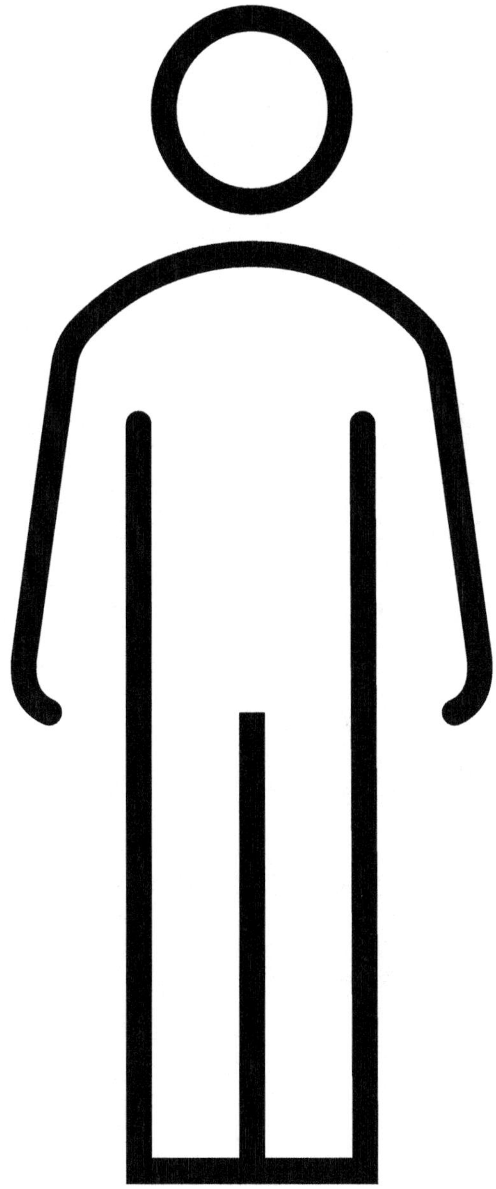

Now, draw your own Avatar!

DID WE COVER EVERYTHING?

Covering everything is not possible. The Chief of Staff role is so nuanced, it can also vary depending on areas of expertise each person brings to the role. It can vary based on the industry, organization size, and so many other factors that can shift role responsibilities, priorities, and expert skills needed for the job.

"It's like flipping through TV channels, and seeing your role being played on each station."

As my Executive Coach once told me, when you're going through a career transition it's good to imagine yourself flipping through the TV and envisioning yourself in each show.

But, as a COS, you're not going through a career transition. This is your life. Being able to keep up with every channel, at every moment, knowing the actors, the script, and keeping track that each show is a hit!

Let's put all these skills you've been reminded of or learned through this booklet to work!

BUT WAIT!

There's More!

Act on this special offer today, and you'll enjoy free shipping too!

JUST KIDDING...

ABOUT THE SHIPPING

But there is more.

Now, you know the WHAT...

but... WHAT about the HOW?

The purpose of this booklet was to walk you through the ins and outs of the WHAT when it comes to the Chief of Staff and executive operations function. Hopefully, something you have learned provided that "AHA!" moment for you and clarified why some of us have enormous respect and confidence in what an established COS brings to an executive team.

THE HOW

Contact Leigh at:

www.COSLeadersCircle.com

Interested in learning more about how to implement the strategies outlined throughout this handbook?

Here you have access to online learning and consulting services to help you implement structure and rigor into your business, while having fun along the way!

Custom Templates **Product Roadmaps** **Events**

Online Courses **Leadership Team Facilitation**

Strategy Reviews

Executive Coaching **Job Shadowing** **Keynotes**

Building Partnerships **COS Recruiting Assessments**

Executive Communications

ROB Framework Development

...so much more!

Program Building

www.COSLeadersCircle.com

LOOK OUT FOR MORE TO COME!

Courses and hands-on consulting in the following areas:

- ✓ COS a Critical Role to Prioritize
- ✓ Defining the Role and Setting Boundaries
- ✓ The Invaluable Impact You Will Have
- ✓ How a COS Defines Strategy
- ✓ Aligning the Organization's Strategy
- ✓ Developing and Implementing OKRs
- ✓ Facilitating Strategic Planning Sessions
- ✓ Building Effective SLT Relationships
- ✓ Managing Executive Communications
- ✓ Establishing Trust and Credibility
- ✓ Managing Up and Across the Organization
- ✓ Building Relationships with Stakeholders
- ✓ Managing Internal Messaging
- ✓ Multi-Project Management Execution
- ✓ Leading Complex Projects
- ✓ Effective Delegation
- ✓ Managing the Office of the CEO
- ✓ Step-by-Step to Your ROB
- ✓ EA AWESOME Network
- ✓ Driving Results and Measuring Success
- ✓ Directly Supporting the CEO's Success
- ✓ How to Think About Time Management
- ✓ Facilitating Meetings and Events
- ✓ Building a High-Performing C Office
- ✓ Hiring, Training, and Developing
- ✓ COS Leader Executive Coaching
- ✓ Measuring the Impact of the COS Role
- ✓ The Future of the Chief of Staff Role
- ✓ An Evolving Function and Title
- ✓ Tools and Templates for Your Toolkit
- ✓ Leadership Team Offsite Success

"Being a Chief of Staff is more than a role – it's a calling to serve and empower leaders to achieve greatness. There's nothing more fulfilling than being a trusted advisor, a strategic partner, and a catalyst for change. It's an honor and a privilege to be a Chief of Staff, and I love MOST minutes of it."

– Leigh Felton

Did I come across a little biased?

Probably. I believe the COS role is one of the least known leadership positions in the company. It can be used as a "doer" rather than a "creator" and this does the organization a disservice. The primary purpose of this book is to drive attention to the importance and potential advancements bringing on the right COS, with the right seniority and responsibilities can do for an organization. Let's talk about it if you disagree!

Not so fast. There is never an "end" to learning as a Chief of Staff. There is always changing technologies, changing best-practices, changing stakeholders and key influentials. And, most important of all, there is certainly the opportunity to grow, collaborate, and enable the best COS leader possible.

BOOK REFLECTIONS

What's Next for You?

Where do you have capability gaps
(either yourself or your organization)?

Good Luck!

Written

by Leigh Felton

Edited

by Leigh Felton

Designed

by Leigh Felton

Graphic Compilations

by Leigh Felton

...because a COS can do it ALL?

OKAY...

You might have found a typo.
Cosly's head placement might not have been in the most complimentary of positions.
The text was too light...
The numbers too small...

YES, I did consider accessibility

(very important to me personally!)

I never said a Chief of Staff is perfect, I just said we TRY to do it all!

Thanks for visiting!

Printed in Great Britain
by Amazon

20891663R00106